Dancing

Kate Castle
Illustrated by Annabel Spenceley

Kingfisher Books

Parents: these notes are for you

From about two and a half years of age, children are ready for dance classes – usually when they are happy to be left on their own for a short while.

Most classes last between half and three quarters of an hour. The class will begin quietly, encouraging the children to stand still and listen to instructions. It will become more and more energetic, but a good teacher will arrange a quiet activity to calm the children down before they go home. Most classes end with the children thanking the teacher with a bow or curtsey, or with a leaving song.

It is easy to see how, for the under-fives, working with other children and learning to watch and listen all develop valuable skills and confidence in preparation for school.

Dance, with its repetition of simple sequences, helps develop memory and co-ordination. For this reason, dance is particularly helpful for disabled and partially-hearing or partially-sighted children. Most classes welcome such children.

Kingfisher Books, Grisewood & Dempsey Ltd
Elsley House, 24–30 Great Titchfield Street, London W1P 7AD

First published in 1990 by Kingfisher Books

Copyright © Grisewood & Dempsey Ltd 1990
All rights reserved

BRITISH LIBRARY CATALOGUING IN PUBLICATION DATA
Castle, Kate
　Dancing.
　1. Dancing – For schools
　I. Title　II. Spenceley, Annabel　III. Series
　793.3
ISBN 0 86272 530 5

Edited by Camilla Hallinan
Cover design by The Pinpoint Design Company
Colour separations by Scantrans Pte Ltd, Singapore
Phototypeset by Southern Positives and Negatives (SPAN)
Printed in Spain

CONTENTS

Ready to go	4
What to wear	6
At the class	8
First steps	10
Moving to music	12
Getting it right	14
On your toes	16
A dance to practise	18
Watching dance	20
Putting on a show	22
What next?	24

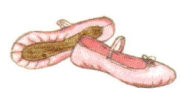

• *Ready to go* •

Dancing is fun. You can dance almost anywhere,

at home and out of doors,

even splish-splashing along the beach.

• *Ready to go* •

You can dance with your friends,

and to stories and rhymes. Can you make the mouse run up the clock?

*Hickory dickory dock,
The mouse ran up the clock;
The clock struck one,
The mouse ran down,
Hickory dickory dock.*

You can learn to dance at a dancing class.

Most children enjoy dancing to the television or radio at home, or joining in action rhymes at playgroup, and will enjoy a dance class too. But it is the shy or clumsy child who can really benefit most from a weekly dance sesson.

 • *What to wear* •

What's in the bag? Clothes for dancing in. You'll need comfortable stretchy clothes so that you can move easily.

You couldn't dance in these clothes. They would be too hot and uncomfortable.

Some dance classes like children to wear special dance clothes.

• *What to wear* •

Instead, you can wear

tracksuit bottoms

a T-shirt

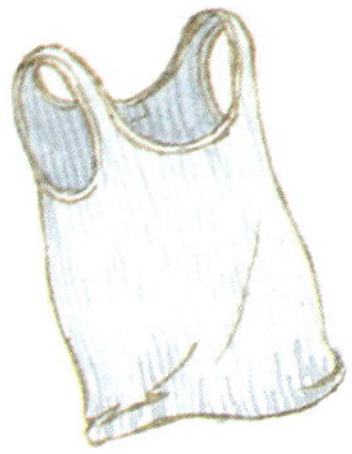

a vest

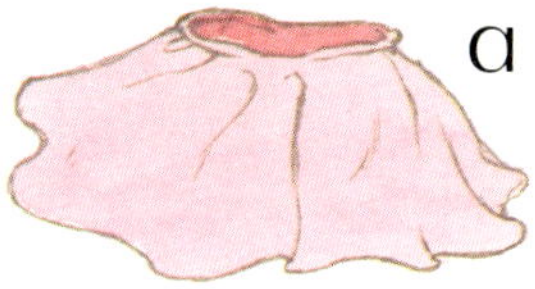

a skirt

shorts

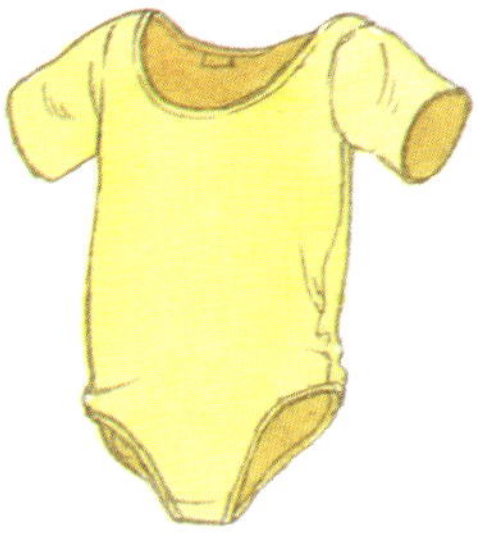

a leotard

short cotton socks

tights

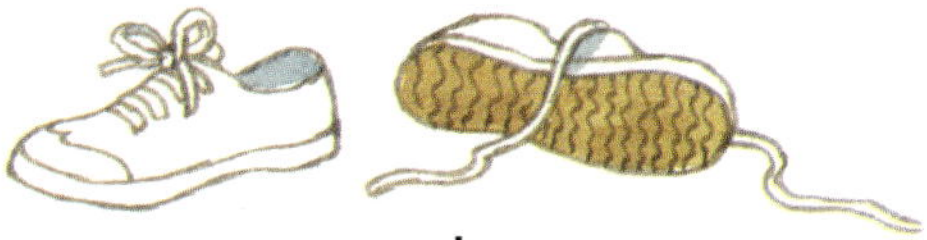

gym shoes

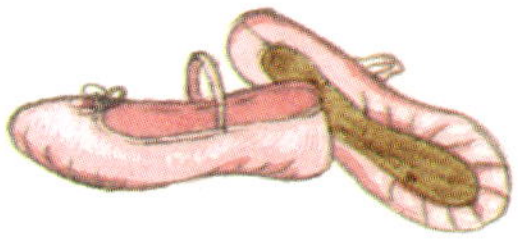

soft dancing shoes with elastics on

or bare feet!

Before you buy anything, find out what your child is expected to wear. Most dance classes insist on tidy hair and comfortable clothes, but some have a special outfit which children will enjoy wearing.

• *At the class* •

It's time to get changed for the dance class.

Girls can put their hair up.

Parents will probably not be encouraged to watch the class, except when a child is very fretful or reluctant. Usually the teacher can cope well with any tears, which normally stop the minute a parent is out of sight. There will often be an open class at the end of term when parents can watch and be pleasantly surprised at their child's progress.

• At the class •

Is teddy ready?

• *First steps* •

At the beginning of the class, you stand quietly, feet together and hands still, listening to the teacher and ready to begin.

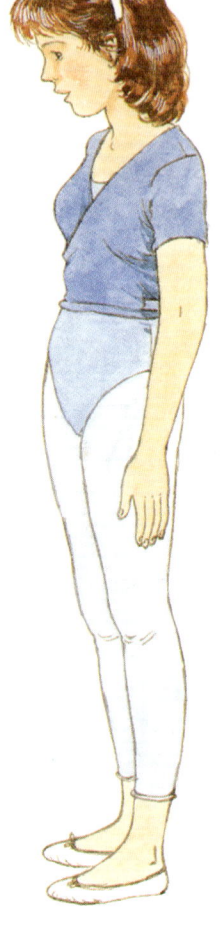

Then you curl up very small,

stretch up very tall,

and ride a galloping horse.

10

• First steps •

Can you roar like a tiger
with fierce teeth and claws?

Stretch and purr
like a sleek cat?

Or swim like
a goldfish?

What else can
you be?

Perhaps you
can walk
on tiptoe,
straight and
strong, with a
golden crown
on your head.

11

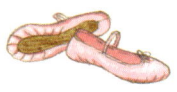

• *Moving to music* •

During the class, the teacher plays music. Listen carefully, and clap your hands in time.

The teacher bangs the tambourine loudly and you go stamp stamp stamp.

If she taps it lightly, you run quickly and quietly on tip-toe.

A pianist is a great help during the class, but taped music can be used just as effectively.

You can help at home between lessons. Try singing nursery rhymes together, with actions and clapping. Play excerpts from a wide range of music. Encourage your child to explore different ways of moving – changing direction, contrasting fast and slow movements and using different parts of the body.

• Moving to music •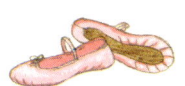

When sitar music plays you can twinkle your fingers like stars and make your hands swim like little fish.

You can rock your baby to sleep with quiet, gentle music . . .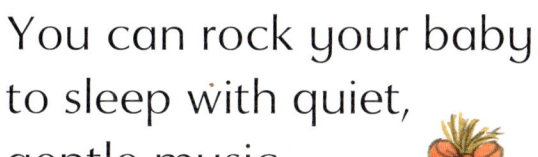

How would you dance to big noisy drums?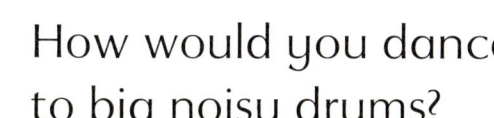

With bells on your ankles you can make your own music when you gallop and skip and hop.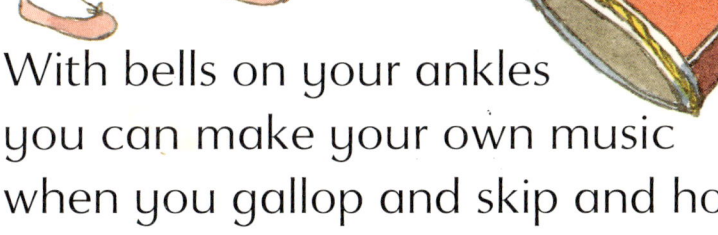

• *Getting it right* •

Watch the teacher carefully and you'll soon get it right.

These exercises are fun to do.
First, you stand tall, with tummies in!

Can you put your hands on your head

shoulders

elbows

• *Getting it right* •

Now the teacher shows you how to point your toes.

Toes can point down – "good toes!"

or up – "bad toes!"

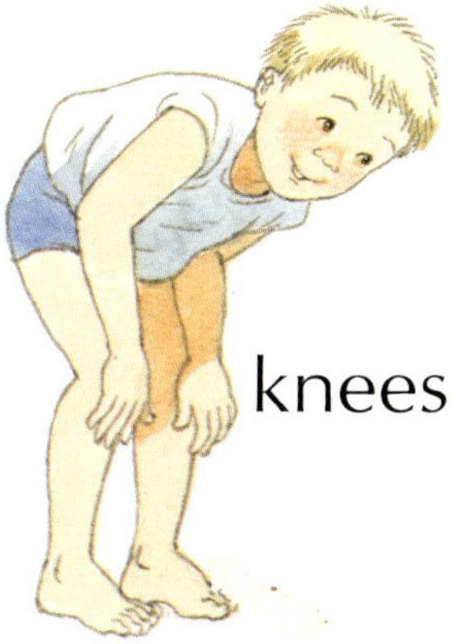

knees

little fingers

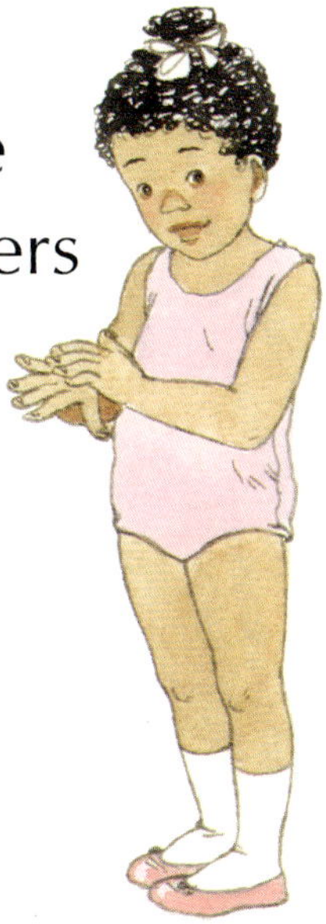

and big toes?

15

First you point your right foot and then your left foot. Do you know which is which?

Here are two ballet positions to try.
Point your toes.

retiré   *pointe tendue*

• On your toes •

Now you all face the same way and skip . . .

Whoops!

Then you dance together. Take hands with your partner and point your toes as you skip.

17

• *A dance to practise* •

This is the story of the hurt bird. Tell it with dance instead of words.

1. One day you are walking through the park.

2. You find a little bird, hiding in the grass. You pick it up, carefully.

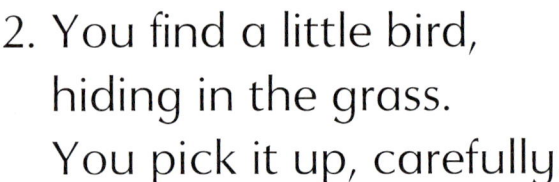

3. Stroke its head, very gently – it is frightened.

4. The bird isn't badly hurt, so you lift it up to the sky, to help it fly away.

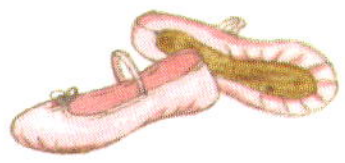

• *A dance to practise* •

5. It is safe now, so jump and clap your hands.

6. Then run and fly like a bird with big strong wings.

At the end of the dance do a curtsey or make a bow.

Do you find that sometimes your feet just won't do as they're told?

• *Watching dance* •

It's fun to watch people dancing. There are many different kinds of dance to watch. You can learn them too.

Some children learn ballet.

• Watching dance •

Some children learn tap dance, in shoes with steel tips that make a noise,

Spanish flamenco,

Irish step dancing, in lace-up shoes,

Russian dance,

and disco!

Indian dance,

At first all young children dance in much the same way. As time goes on, they may want to specialize by learning a particular style.

Offer your child the opportunity to see as much dance as possible. Although full-length ballets at the theatre are probably too demanding at this age, short programmes and special introductory matinées are ideal.

• *Putting on a show* •

You can go to the theatre to watch dance, and you can be part of a show yourself.

It's fun to show how well you can dance. Practise each week until you can dance really well.

Would you like to dance in The Three Little Pigs, or in another story?

• What next? •

Look for classes in arts, leisure and sports centres as well as specialist dance studios. Cultural associations such as Afro-Caribbean, Chinese and Asian groups offer sessions in these dance forms. Some Local Authorities employ a dance worker to organize classes and workshops on a more informal basis. Several dance companies also offer workshops geared to this age-group. Your local library is also a good source of information about pre-school activities. Nursery and infant schools should offer dance on the curriculum, usually creative or country dancing. Some playgroups run parent and toddler sessions where you can dance alongside your child.

Here are some useful addresses for further information about dance classes:

ADITI
(National Association of South Asian Dancers)
7th Floor, Jacob's Well
Bradford BD1 5RW
0274 754090

Black Dance Development Trust
Princes Chambers, Rooms 43–46
6 Corporation Street
Birmingham B2 4RN
021-631 3808

British Ballet Organisation
Woolborough House
39 Lonsdale Road
London SW13 9JP
01-748 1241

Council for Dance Education and Training
5, Tavistock Place
London WC1H 9SN
01-388 5770

English Folk Dance and Song Society
Cecil Sharpe House
2 Regents Park Road
London NW1 7AY
01-485 2206

The Imperial Society of Teachers of Dancing
Euston Hall
Birkenhead Street
London WC1H 8BE
01-837 9967

International Dance Teachers' Association
76 Bennett Road
Brighton BN2 5JL
0273-685652

Royal Academy of Dancing
48 Vicarage Crescent
London SW11 3LT
01-223 0091

SHAPE
(for information on opportunities for the disabled)
1 Thorpe Close
London W10 5XL
01-960 9245

Sports Council
(parent & toddler movement classes)
16 Upper Woburn Place
London WC1H 0PQ
01-388 1277

Other books to read
For children:

The **Angelina Ballerina** series
Helen Craig and Katharine Holabird
Aurum Books for Children/Picture Puffin

The Dancing Class
Helen Oxenbury *Walker Books*

Little Box of Ballet Stories
Francesca Crespi
Methuen Children's Books Ltd

My Ballet Class
Rachel Isadora *Fontana Picture Lion*

For parents:

Dancing Games for Children of All Ages
Ester Nelson *Sterling Publishing*

Look! Look What I Can Do!
Creative Action Ideas for Under Sevens
Kate Harrison *BBC Books*

Joy of Dancing
Sonia Chamberlain
Royal Academy of Dancing
(principally for teachers)

24